Fire on the Farm

Story by
Pauline Cartwright

Illustrated by
Julian Bruère

Rigby PM Collection and PM Plus

Emerald Level 25

U.S. Edition © 2013 HMH Supplemental Publishers
10801 N. MoPac Expressway
Building #3
Austin, TX 78759
www.hmhsupplemental.com

Text © 2003 Cengage Learning Australia Pty Limited
Illustrations © 2003 Cengage Learning Australia Pty Limited
Originally published in Australia by Cengage Learning Australia

14   1957   16
4500601371

Text: Pauline Cartwright
Illustrations: Julian Bruère
Printed in China by 1010 Printing International Ltd

Fire on the Farm
ISBN 978 0 75 784124 8

Contents

Chapter 1

Fire in the Distance

"Remember you can reach us on Dad's cell phone if you're worried about anything," called Mom, as Dad turned the car toward the farm gate. The fierce wind whipped up the dust behind the car, and the two children shielded their eyes. "We'll be at the bank for an hour or so. And you're going to make the salad for dinner. Now don't forget."

Shannon knew that Mom was talking to her, not Toby. She did forget things quite often. Sometimes Dad got mad at her. At other times, he gave her a hug and told her she was a dreamer and that he supposed that the world needed dreamers.

Now, while she was in charge, even if it was only for two hours, she must not forget anything.

"Give me a turn on the phone," said Toby, reaching for their mom's cell phone.

Shannon thrust the phone behind her back. "Dad told me to keep it with me all afternoon. You know he doesn't like to leave us alone, even for an urgent meeting with the bank manager."

"Don't be so bossy," moaned her brother. "I just want to call Peter Campbell about soccer."

"Well, go and call him on the house phone," said Shannon.

Toby made a face at her and walked off.

Shannon sat on the swing that hung from the old oak tree. Tip and Black, the farm dogs, watched her. The wind was making them restless. It seemed as if the wind, wild overhead, might blow the tree over. But Dad had said the oak tree roots went down deep. This could be why it still had green leaves, although the leaves of the birches in the other corner of the yard were dropping already. It was the driest summer for years.

"I can't bear to see the trees die," Mom had said. "I *hate* this drought."

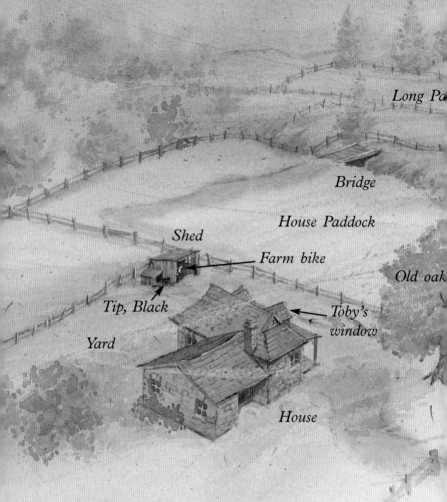

Long Pa

Bridge

House Paddock

Shed

Farm bike

Old oak

Tip, Black

Toby's window

Yard

House

Shannon looked past the frizzled garden with its rock-hard soil to the farmland beyond. She thought the sun-gold grass had a kind of beauty. But, beautiful or not, the dry stalks were useless for grazing sheep.

She had wanted to cry at the look on Dad's face when he had to sell his sheep. And she had crept quietly away the day she found her mother crying over a pile of bills on the kitchen table. At least they had been able to keep the three horses.

Suddenly, guiltily, Shannon thought of the horse gate. When she checked the horses' water supply that morning, had she shut the gate?

Just then Toby's voice cried out, "Shannon! Quick! Come and look. There's a fire!"

Chapter 2

The Flames Come Fast

As Shannon jumped off the swing, a gust of wind almost knocked her over. She battled toward the house. Panic welled up inside her.

"Hurry, Shannon!" Toby's call came from upstairs.

Shannon looked up and saw him staring through Dad's binoculars. She raced up the stairs, and the wind slammed the door shut behind her.

"Look, Shannon! Look!"

Shannon didn't need binoculars. She could see the billowing smoke, and at its base, moving over the dry, scorched land, a long red zigzag of leaping flames.

It looked as if the fire might have begun back in Winston Valley, which ran from the distant hills to the edge of their farm.

"Look how fast it's coming!" cried Toby. "Toward our farm!"

The wind, thought Shannon. *The wind is driving the flames straight for us.*

"I want Mom and Dad to come home." Toby looked as if he was about to cry.

At that moment the house phone rang.

"Shannon, get me your mom or dad." It was Mrs. Campbell from the farm next door.

Shannon whispered, "They're in town, at the bank."

There was a silence. Then Mrs. Campbell was saying, "Shannon, I don't know if you've seen – "

" Yes, we've seen the fire."

"I'm sending Aaron over to get you."

"I'll call Mom and Dad on Dad's cell phone," said Shannon.

"Good girl. Remember, stay close to the house. Aaron will be there soon."

As she put the phone down, Shannon thought of the horses. She had to do something about the horses.

Chapter 3

No Time for Fear

"Toby, stay here in the house. I want you to do something really important. So no crying, okay?"

Toby swallowed hard and waited.

Shannon handed him the phone. "Call Dad's cell phone. The number is on the wall in his office. You can watch out the window for Aaron Campbell. He's coming to get us."

"Tell Mom and Dad about the fire. And tell them we're going to the Campbells' place. Can you do that?"

"Yes." Toby gripped the phone and glanced out the window. "What are you going to do?"

"I'm going to get the horses."

"You can't! They're in the Pines Paddock. Near the fire!"

"We can't let them burn. They're the only stock Dad has left. I'll take the farm bike and go as fast as I can. I'll just let them out so they can run away from the fire. It'll be all right."

"Shannon, I'm scared."

"You can't be scared!" said Shannon fiercely. "You have to be grown-up, and responsible. Call Mom and Dad. *Now.* Tell them to come home. I'll be back in a few minutes. Watch me out the window." Shannon went across the yard to get the bike.

The wind was wild and gusty, tearing at Shannon's hair. It carried the smell of smoke. For a moment or two, she felt fear rising inside her. From the yard she couldn't see the flames, but she could remember how they looked from upstairs, sliding, like a jagged red snake, over the land.

She knew the flames would frighten the horses and wondered again if she had shut the gate of the Pines Paddock. She tried *so hard* not to forget, but today she hoped she *had* forgotten. If the gate was open, the horses might be loose and she would not have to go so near the fire.

Tip and Black were barking. They knew that danger was near. Shannon undid their chains and ran with them to the house.

"Toby," she yelled, "the dogs will keep you company."

Toby raced down to the door, clutching Mom's phone to his ear. He was stammering a hello into the phone as he pulled the dogs in and shut the door behind them. Shannon whirled away on the three-wheeler toward the fire.

Chapter 4

Save the Horses

Shannon rode carefully. The smoke was closer and the smell stronger. All she could think of was the horses and how much Dad cared about them.

Because the sheep had been sold, the gates were open between the paddocks. She rode across the House Paddock and over the dry creek bed. She glanced ahead to the row of pine trees that gave shelter on one side of the paddock where the horses were. Pine trees would burn easily.

Riding into the strong wind was slowing her down. She had to get there faster. She headed through the gateway into Long Paddock. A sudden movement caught her eye. She glanced ahead.

There they were – Star, Jess, and Aster, galloping across Long Paddock toward her. She *had* left the gate open. Yes, there beyond the horses, she could see it swinging.

Flames at the end of Winston Valley were racing into the dry gold grass of the Pines Paddock. If the gate had been closed, she could not have stopped long enough to get it open. She might have had to leave the horses shut inside. They would have tried to jump fences, but they weren't trained jumpers – they were breeding mares, and they could have injured themselves.

Thank goodness she had forgotten to shut the gate.

Shannon turned the bike and was caught by a huge gust of wind. Even though she had turned right around she still seemed to be battling against it. She should have been riding with the wind now.

The horses were running ahead of her. They had been spooked by the fire. She could see that in the way they moved, whinnying and shying every few yards.

Shannon felt a new worry. They might run for miles. They might get lost. They could end up tangled in fences or on a roadway filled with traffic. She wanted them to follow her back to the house, but she feared they were too skittish and frightened to do that.

Shannon stopped the bike for a moment, and turned her head to look at the progress of the fire. Then she knew why she was still battling against the wind.

A good half of the Pines Paddock was blackened, but on the far side of the black was the zigzag of flame. The wind was pushing the flames away from the row of pines, away from their farm. The wind had changed direction!

Chapter 5

The Danger Is Past

The horses had changed direction, too. They were running back toward Shannon and had slowed their pace.

"You beauties! Come, come! Come, Star. Come, Jess. Come, Aster."

As Shannon called, she rode through Long Paddock and the House Paddock, and, even when a helicopter flew over, heading out to survey the fire, the horses ran beside her.

Perhaps, she thought, they needed someone with them to make them feel safe.

As she rode into the yard, Aaron Campbell's car was coming up the drive and, beyond it, another car – her parents.

"Toby caught us before we reached town," called Dad. He leaped from the car and hugged Shannon and Toby. Mom was close behind. Then Dad saw the horses. He stared past the yard – now filled with people and animals – to the Pines Paddock and the fire beyond.

"You got the horses out." His face was one enormous smile of joy. Shannon felt hot with pleasure and pride.

Once Star, Jess, and Aster were safely enclosed in the Back Paddock, Shannon waved good-bye to her dad as he raced off to help fight the fire. Toby was upstairs watching through the binoculars in case the helicopters returned, carrying huge buckets of water.

Because of the wind change, their farm was safe, but others were still in the path of the fire. Shannon helped Mom make sandwiches that they knew the tired and hungry firefighters would need.

29

Every now and again, Toby called them to look at the fire from the upstairs window. Once Mom said, "Toby, straighten up this room. There are cushions and rugs everywhere. You'd think the dogs had been racing about in here!" She didn't understand why Toby couldn't stop laughing.

In the late afternoon, the wind dropped. Shannon and Toby went to bed that night knowing that the danger was over.

They didn't see Dad until the next morning.

"Shannon," said Dad, putting an arm around her shoulders, "I hope you didn't put yourself in any danger getting the horses out. They're precious to me, but you're more precious, by far. You know that, don't you?"

She had to tell him. She couldn't let him think she'd been braver and cleverer than she really was. Besides, he should know that she would never take risks; had the gate been properly closed she would not have waited to open it with the flames so close. She would have left the horses to jump out as best they could.

Dad listened to her story. "You know, Shannon, people who forget to shut gates can be a farmer's worst nightmare." He smiled. "This is the first and only time I've ever been glad that someone forgot to shut a gate."

Shannon grinned. "I'm getting better at remembering things. So perhaps I'd better make that salad now."

Toby grinned too. "One day late," he reminded her. Then he looked up into the sky. "Hey, I hope someone remembered to shut the upstairs windows. I think it's going to rain."